MW00710745

A Birth in the Family

A Birth in the Family

Nativity Poems

by
Norma Farber

EL LEÓN LITERARY ARTS

Copyright © 2002 by El León Literary Arts, Inc.

No part of this book may be reproduced in any manner
without written permission from the publisher,
except in brief quotations used in article reviews.

A Birth in the Family is published by El León Literary Arts
and distributed by Creative Arts Book Company.
El León Literary Arts is a nonprofit public benefit corporation
established to extend the array of voices essential to a democra-
cy's arts and education. The Overbrook Foundation's generous
support is gratefully acknowledged.

For information contact:
Creative Arts Book Company
833 Bancroft Way
Berkeley, California 94710
1-800-848-7789

ISBN 0-88739-538-4
Library of Congress Catalog Number 2002112480
Printed in the United States of America

A Birth in the Family

GUARDIAN OWL

Company coming by night,
who *are* you? Whoo?
I live here. I have a right
to know what's new.

Then welcome, come so far,
so much ado.
I guard the stable a star
is pointing to.
Enter, the door's ajar,
to fit the fullest of you.

Go in, I'll check you off.
You're overdue.
Don't push or pinch or shove
for a better view.
Just say your name with love
when I ask, Who *are* you? Whoo?

LADYBUG'S CHRISTMAS

From winter sleep,
this waking day,
I crawl six-legged
to a crib of hay.
Make way! Make way!

With dainty speed
I tiptoe, red
as a pomegranate seed,
a holly berry,
a hawthorn bead.

Oh what a sight
for drowsy eyes!
In a sweet hollow
of ample size
a baby lies,

snow-whitely dressed
in his newborn best.
I climb an inch
of infant vest.
I stay a while.

To think I've been
worn like a jewel,
a fiery pin,
a ruby sequin,
over his heart.

[3]

CHIME OF THE SPIDER

I sing no sound. I spin instead.
High in the loft above your head
I weave my quiet song of thread.

I loop my wiring silver-clear
to light your manger chandelier.
Listen! My web is what you hear.

WASN'T IT FINE —

that a black-backed cricket was able
to stay from the end of September
hidden in a stable —
of all surprising places —
through most of December
in time to stand at the manger —
by chance or design —
rubbing his lyric wing-cases
that chirruped Welcome! to every new-
comer kin and neighbor and stranger
and praised the gifts three kings were bringing
and chirruped chirruped till every creature
must carol according to its nature
and chirruped till even the straw was singing?

CAROL OF THE PORCUPINE

Soften every spine,
lessen every quill,
even every odd.

Murmur very low
at this cradleside:
every breath a dew

on a satin blade,
every sharpened spear
a velvet word.

SLOTH, MOSEYING

From the branch of a tree,
a fur hammock's suspended.
That's *me!*

As everyone knows,
I begin to begin to travel
when the wind blows.

From bough to bough to bough,
I move single-handed.
Easy if you know how.

There are swifter mammals. Let *them*
hurry. In my own time
I'm getting to Bethlehem.

I hang on a cross-beam
within the stable: so still
I disturb no one's dream.

I hang as I please
and to please an infant
who will learn about trees.

STORK, BOWING

Up from the Nile I heave
to the holy midst.
I poke my nosey bill
in the way of man and beast.

Over my chimney-nest
I've seen that rumoring star.
What's the news, anyway?
I've come far, far.

Kings, out of my way!
Shepherd, lower your crook.
Creatures, stand aside.
I want a good long look.
O child, I take my fill.
I bow my long stork bill.

HARK, THE DOVE

What thing
should I sing,
little king?
    Coo-roo

What dear word
of a bird
should be heard?
    Coo-roo?

What save love
can a dove
carol of?
    Coo-roo!

ROOSTER CHEER

Cock-a-doodle-do!
I'd rather crow than coo.

I'd rather crow for Mary's son
than ring a belfry carillon.

I'd rather gather manger grain
than be a golden weather-vane.

CATERPILLAR CAROL

Softer than the breath of woolly bears,
      sleeping:
the sound of my velvet bellows,
      creeping.
Quieter than woolly bears stretching,
      bending:
the carol of my concertina,
      wending.

LAMP IN THE MANGER

Let the glowworms come inside
close to one another.
Let them be a lamp beside
a baby and his mother.

Let them with each tiny flare
light the baby's features
like a torch illumined there
for the gathered creatures.

Loud in heaven a starry glow
burns for Christmas glory.
Let these little fires below
bank a quiet story.

HOG'S GIFT

Shall Hog with holy child converse?
How will it feel?

Jesu dear,
I lumber near.

You may yank my tail,
pull my ear.

I'll make you a small
silk purse.

COUSIN ARMADILLO

Were you there when the lovely boy was born?
Did you waddle toward the manger like a lamp
through the splended host, to take your rightful turn?

Did they laugh at you behind their lifted paws?
Did they clear their throat behind their cloaking wing?
Did they stare you down as though they dared refuse
to let you spend your moment at the crib?
Did you shut your naked ears to what they said:
"Just a turtle-shell around a baby pig!"

Did you lumber on and reach the shining hay
where the mother watched the infant at her side
and the infant watched the crowding company?

Did you notice what pure light the child lay in?
How he stirred in your direction — didn't he?
And was seen to smile and welcome you as kin?

MOOSE AT THE MANGER

I have to bend my head
to get in at the stable door.

I live under northen ceilings.
I'm used to a piney floor.

I like the smell of this barn,
the sound of animal chorus,

the sight of hay and infant —
I've never seen either before.

Let him lie on a fleece on my antlers.
He rides and I adore.

LION, KNEELING

Bye, baby Jesu,
look who's come to please you,
come to doff his tawny skin
to wrap a brand-new baby in.

Waken merry. Touch and see.

Jesu, you have company.

TURTLE TOWARD BETHLEHEM

I'm slow as molasses.
That's me, that's my nature.
From every last creature
Bethlehem bound who passes,
I'm begging a lift.
Lion sweeps by, oh he's swift!
Lamb right beside him.
Camel comes loping.
I holler from under my shell. I'm hoping
he'll ask me to ride him.

Some things won't wait.
I need to be there while the baby's still new.
Nest summer won't do.
Today in the stable they gather to celebrate.
Later — who knows?
Amazing how fast an infant grows.
Amazing this Ram, with horns in his bonnet.
How tempting his back!
I wish I could scramble up on it.
I haven't the knack.

Please get me to the manger on time!
Galumphing Baboon.
Big Bull, Brown Beaver, Cinnamon Bear,
Not one with a second to spare —
not Cony, not Coon.
Who are these three?

They're *Kings!* They're stopping Stooping.
For *me?*
They're knotting their cloaks together.
They're making
a hammock. O joy!
Am I dreaming a dream, or waking?
I'm coming, sweet boy.

I'm getting to the manger on time!

ALL THOSE MOTHERS AT THE MANGER

All those mothers at the manger,
hen and cow and mare and ewe,
gathered round the lovely stranger
while her baby still was new.

All those mothers at the manger,
cow and mare and ewe and hen,
welcomed warm the lovely stranger,
welcomed soft her baby then.

All those mothers at the manger,
mare and ewe and hen and cow,
praised the lovely stranger:
perfect features, peaceful brow.

All those mothers at the manger,
ewe and hen and cow and mare,
said, "No mother is a stranger
to another anywhere!"

MARY, DID YOU FALTER?

Mary, did you falter
that early hour
when seed took shelter
in your womb's core?

Mary, were you sickened
with right unrest
as seedling thickened,
yourself increased?

Mary, did you startle
at wingwind heard
under your girdle:
rustle of bird?

Mary, were you swollen
to proud distress,
excelling, telling
your Mary-ness?

Your brow, was it ashened
as more you bore?
And were you impatient
as women are?

Mary, did you murmur
of marvel then
when need made clamor,
when milk came in?

Mary, weary Mary,
did you cry out
in disorder and glory
for babe complete?

And did you lean over
the child in arm,
and wish him never
to grow to man?

CROOKED CAROL

Mary had a baby:
good news!
Red as a ruby,
but no layette, no shoes.

Who's to be godfather?
Joseph, maybe?
Solemn, he nods
his step-paternity

over the rude crib.
How refuse?
Mary had a baby:
sing *Whose! Whose!*

THE FOUNDLING

Wasn't it strange
when I held up the baby to Joseph
who saw its hair a halo
and cupped the head and searched
the holy face for resemblance —
dear God! — to his own?

Was it surprising
he missed the family traits
and found the child a sun
so luminous, he wavered
with light-blindness, and wept
for a son of his own?

EASY ENOUGH FOR STRANGERS

Easy enough for strangers —
far-come and famous kings —
to lavish a child
with weathy offerings.

How shall I help his mother
Mary, my sweet wife,
raise him up to a long,
abundant life?

How teach him true reward,
how tell him cost?
How be father
to a boy star-crossed?

THE QUEENS CAME LATE

The Queens came late, but the Queens were there
with gifts in their hands and crowns in their hair.
They'd come, these three, like Kings, from afar,
following, yes, that guiding star.
They'd left their ladles, linens, looms,
their children playing in nursery rooms,
and told their sitters: "Take charge! For this
is a marvelous sight we must not miss!"

The Queens came late, but not too late
to see the animals small and great,
feathered and furred, domestic and wild,
gathered to gaze at a mother and child.
And rather than frankincense and myrrh
and gold for the babe, they brought for her
who held him, a homespun gown of blue,
and chicken soup — with noodles, too —
and a lingering, lasting cradle-song.

The Queens came late and stayed not long,
for their thoughts already were straining far —
past manger and mother and guiding star
and child a-glow as a morning star —
toward home and children and chores undone.

FAR, FAR FROM BETHLEHEM

I never went to Bethlehem.
I stayed right here. I plumped a goose,
put up preserves, measured a hem,
retrieved a piglet, running loose.

I washed the laundry, hung it neat,
then I took it down by dark of day,
and folded it and laid it, sweet
and fresh for further use, away.

I never got to Bethlehem.
Someone, I thought, should (day *and* night)
be here, someone should stay at home.
I think I probably was right.

For I have sung my child to dream
far, far away from where there lies
a woman doing much the same.
And neither of our children cries.

HAD I BEEN THERE, THAT MANGER DATE

Had I been there, that manger date,
would she have bid me take the child
and lay him close against my heart
and press him nestled on my shoulder?

Would she have let me, like an aunt,
cup the sweet head within my palm
as though it were a rarest plant
I must support to keep it blooming?

Would she have watched alert with care
for kiss too rude, embrace too swift,
for finger brushed along his hair
too near the newborn coin of softness?

And would she fret in emptiness
as though I were the world that took
too much from her, and cry her loss
with *That's enough,* and take him back?

COME LEARN OF MARY

Who can't rejoice,
come learn of me,
that hold a baby
on my knee,
and keep him safe
for what's to be.

CAROL OF THE CHRISTMAS MUSHROOM

The woods have dropped mute.
December's old.
Come again on velvet foot,
collybia of the cold.

Come tawny in a tuft of song,
Stand soft, carol lowly
as the least bangle
fallen from a Christmas tree.

Sing rounds of thaw. Sing ochre
coinage of earth.
Tide the hoar-foraging folk
to an edible weath.

Grounding of good news:
proclaim away frost
and frondose snows.
Hosanna the forest!

GREEN CHRISTMAS

This narrow month of winter
when most we huddle close,
let trees stand in our center,
boughs broaden our house.

Let forests arise from floors,
stems commingle with men:
walls shall go out of doors
as verdant woods come in.

How rims of ceiling unfurl
reaching a range unused.
Branches largen the hall.
dimensions are disenclosed.

Proper the dwellings wherever
are sheltered the far-fetched plants,
the tracts brought in under cover:
green be this residence.

MANGER MEMENTO

Here's a silken straw,
one of a hundredfold
that once in winter lay
under a dreaming child

and let him rest
softer than usual hay
allows the farmer's beast
roughly to lie.

He slept unruffled,
he woke in light.
Here's a reminder.
Remember it.

B. Whipple

Poet, concert singer, actress, novelist, translator; wife, mother, grandmother, widow. Norma Farber (1909-1984) was the author of more than thirty books. Her poems appeared in periodicals including *The Christian Science Monitor, The Nation, The New Yorker,* and *The New York Times*. In the manger story, Norma Farber found the purity and potential which the birth of any child may signify, as well as the enchantment that compelled creatures of field and forest. Illustrated by artists including Petra Mathers, and set to music by composers including Daniel Pinkham, the nativity poems of Norma Farber continue to bring alive this extraordinary moment of harmony and promise.